Mises in America

William H. Peterson

Mises in America

William H. Peterson

LvMI

MISES INSTITUTE

Published 2018 by the Ludwig von Misees Institute.
This work is licensed under a Creative Commons
Attribution-NonCommercial-NoDerivs 4.0 International
License. *http://creativecommons.org/licenses/by-nc-nd/4.0*

Ludwig von Mises Institute
518 West Magnolia Ave
Auburn, AL 36832
Mises.org.

ISBN: 978-1-933550-42-8

Contents

Introduction

William Peterson is sometimes regarded as among Ludwig von Mises's most prolific students. This is a great credit to Professor Peterson because it is not precisely true. Peterson received his Masters degree from Columbia in 1948, and his Ph.D. from New York University (1953) but not from entirely studying under Mises. Instead he met Mises while teaching at New York University.

He was a colleague of Mises's, not a student as such. Peterson received a conventional education in mainstream theory, and became a Misesian under Mises's influence at Mises's own seminar led by Murray Rothbard. So it was his willingness to change his mind, to learn from a colleague, to delve into a new research program following his formal education, that led Peterson to be one of the leading spokesmen for the free market during his long career.

These are rare qualities in an academic economist. Rarer still is his capacity for clarity of expression and soundness of principle, which he has shown throughout his life. The essays contained in this book illustrate the point beautifully. Few have written so poetically about the capacity of the market economy to bring social peace and prosperity in a manner that reveals the true preferences of its society's members. The market is the best and more authentic form of true democracy, a point he has made throughout his life.

In 2005 he was given the Gary G. Schlarbaum Award for Lifetime Achievement in the Cause of Human Liberty. He has taught at the University of Tennessee at Chattanooga, and Campbell University in North Carolina, where he influenced thousands of students. He was chief economist for U.S. Steel and worked for the U.S. Department of Commerce. His articles can be found in the *New York Times*, the *Harvard Business Review*, *Business Week*, the *Journal of Economic Literature*, and many other places. For fourteen years, he wrote regular columns for the *Wall Street Journal*. He has spoken at every opportunity around the country to students and faculty and businesspeople.

All the while, he has worked to draw people's attention to Mises and his thought, presenting it in a way that is compelling and persuasive. In many ways, this is an act of great humility and piety—again, a highly unusual combination for an economist of his stature and accomplishment. It is no wonder that he became such a dear friend of both Ludwig and Margit von Mises, as well as just about every other pro-liberty thinker of the second half of the twentieth century.

Mises was not the only benefactor of Peterson's work. He has reviewed thousands of books, and celebrated other great figures in the history of liberty, from Jefferson to Hazlitt. He has been driven by a passion to get the word out, and somehow make a contribution to alerting the world to great ideas that have been unjustly ignored. In so doing, he has made a great difference.

It is long past time for Peterson to be celebrated in his own right, as both a man and an intellectual force. After a lifetime of drawing attention to others, it is a thrill to see this collection in print, in the hope that it can turn the spotlight on Peterson himself, whose extraordinary gifts to the world will long endure.

Llewellyn H. Rockwell, Jr.
March 2009

Ludwig von Mises: Thoughts and Memories

A generation of students at New York University's graduate business school who took the economics courses of Ludwig von Mises remember a gentle, diminutive, soft-spoken, white-haired, European scholar—with a mind like a steel trap.

Mises, who celebrated his 90th birthday on September 29, 1971, is an uncompromising rationalist and one of the world's great thinkers. He has built his philosophical edifice on freedom and free enterprise and on reason and individuality. He starts with the premise that the concept of economic man is pure fiction—that man is a whole being with his thought and action tightly

This essay was first published in *Toward Liberty* (Menlo Park, Calif.: Institute for Humane Studies, 1971), pp. 268–73. Note: All page references to *Human Action* are to the Scholar's Edition (Auburn, Ala.: Ludwig von Mises Institute, [1988] 2008).

integrated into cause and effect. All this is sub-
sumed under the title of his 900-page *magnum
opus*, *Human Action*, first published in 1949.

Mises, a total anti-totalitarian and Distinguished Fellow of the American Economic Association, was a professor of political economy at
New York University for a quarter-century, retir-
ing in 1969. Before that he had a professorship
at the Graduate Institute of International Studies
in Geneva. And before Geneva he had long been
a professor at the University of Vienna—a professorship which the Nazis' *Anschluss* takeover
of Austria, understandably, terminated. Among
his students in Vienna were Gottfried Haberler,
Friedrich Hayek, and Fritz Machlup. Profes-
sors Haberler of Harvard and Machlup of Princeton have each been presidents of the American
Economic Association; Hayek is an economic
scholar of world renown.

Starting right after World War II, Mises gave
three courses at NYU: "Socialism and the Profit
System," "Government Control and the Profit
System," and "Seminar in Economic Theory." In
each course he carefully established the primacy
of freedom in the marketplace. He stated that the
unhampered pricing mechanism, ever pulling
supply and demand toward equilibrium but never
quite reaching it, is the key to resource optimization and, indirectly, to a free and creative society.

Mises believes in choice. He believes that choosing determines all human decisions and hence the entire sphere of human action—a sphere he designates as "praxeology." He holds that the types of national economies prevailing across the world and throughout history have been simply the outcome of various means intellectually, if not always appropriately, chosen to achieve certain ends. His litmus test is the extent of the market; accordingly, he distinguishes broadly among three types of economies: capitalism, socialism and the so-called middle way—government intervention in the marketplace.

Mises believes in government but limited, noninterventionist government. He wrote in *Human Action*:

> The issue is not *automatism versus conscious action*; it is *autonomous action of each individual versus the exclusive action of the government.* It is *freedom vs. government omnipotence.* (p. 726)

He believes that while the vast majority of men generally concur on ends, men very frequently differ on governmental means—sometimes with cataclysmic results, as in the various applications of extreme socialism in fascism and communism, or of extreme interventionism in other types of economies, "mixed" or socialist.

Mises reasons that regardless of the type of economy the tough, universal economic problem for the individual in both his personal and political capacities is ever to reconcile ends and choose among means, rationally and effectively. Free, i.e., non-coerced, individual choice is the key to personal and societal development if not survival, he argues, and intellectual freedom and development are keys to effective choices. He declared: "Man has only one tool to fight error—reason."

Mises, well aware of the unlearned lessons of history, thus sees something of an either-or human destiny. While man could destroy himself and civilization, he could also ascend to undreamed-of cultural, intellectual and technological heights. In any event, thought would be decisive. Mises believes in the free market of ideas as well as of goods and services—in the potential of the human intellect.

The nature of this leader of the Austrian School of economics can be seen in an incident during a conference of the Mont Pèlerin Society, an international group of scholars dedicated to the principles of a free society, meeting in Seelisburg, Switzerland in 1949. Mises expressed fear that some of the members were themselves becoming inadvertently infected by the virus of intervention—minimum wages, social insurance, contra-cyclical fiscal policy, etc.

"But what would you do," it was put to him, "if you were in the position of our French colleague,

Jacques Rueff?" who was present and at the time responsible for the fiscal administration of Monaco. "Suppose there were widespread unemployment and hence famine and revolutionary discontent in the principality. Would you advise the government to limit its activities to police action for the maintenance of order and the protection of private property?"

Mises was intransigent. He responded: "If the policies of nonintervention prevailed—free trade, freely fluctuating wage rates, no form of social insurance, etc.—there would be no acute unemployment. Private charity would suffice to prevent the absolute destitution of the very restricted hard core of unemployables."

The failure of socialism, according to Mises, lay in its inherent inability to attain sound "economic calculation." He argued in his 1922 work, *Socialism*, published five years after the Bolshevik Revolution that shook the world, that Marxist economics lacked an effective means for "economic calculation"—i.e., an adequate substitute for the critical resource-allocation function of the market pricing mechanism. Thus socialism is inherently self-condemned to inefficiency, unable to expeditiously register supply and demand forces and consumer preferences in the marketplace.

Some years later, Oskar Lange, then of the University of California and later chief economic planner of Poland's Politburo, recognized the challenge of the Mises critique on socialist

economic calculation. So he in turn challenged
the socialists to somehow devise an allocative
system to duplicate the efficiency of market
allocation. He even proposed a statue in honor
of Mises to acknowledge the invaluable service
the leader of the Austrian School had presum-
ably rendered to the cause of socialism in directing attention to this as yet unsolved question in
socialist theory. However, notwithstanding some
slight shifts of the Polish, Soviet, and other Eastern European countries toward freer economics,
a statue of Mises has yet to be erected in War-
saw's main square.

But probably to Mises the more immediate
economic threat to the West is not so much exter-
nal communism as internal interventionism—
government ever undermining, if not outrightly
supplanting, the marketplace. Interventionism
from public power production to farm price sup-
ports, from pushing minimum wages up to forcing interest rates down, from vigorously expand-
ing credit to contracting, however inadvertently,
capital formation. Citing German interventionist
experience of the 1920s climaxing in the Hitle-
rian regime and British interventionism of the
post-World War II era culminating in devaluations
and economic decline, he holds such so-called
middle-of-the-road policies that sooner or later
lead to some form of collectivism, whether of the
socialist, fascist, or communist mold.

He maintains economic interventionism necessarily produces friction whether at home or, as in the cases of foreign aid and international commodity agreements, abroad. What otherwise would be simply the voluntary action of private citizens in the marketplace becomes coercive and politicized intervention when transferred to the public sector. Such intervention breeds more intervention. Animosity and strain, if not outright violence, become inevitable. Property and contract are weakened, militancy and revolution are strengthened.

In time, inevitable internal conflicts could be "externalized" into warfare. Mises holds in *Human Action*:

> In the long run war and the preservation of the market economy are incompatible. Capitalism is essentially a scheme for peaceful nations. . . . To defeat the aggressors is not enough to make peace durable. The main thing is to discard the ideology that generates war. (pp. 824, 828)

But what if a peaceful nation is nonetheless plunged into inflation-inducing war? Surely then it should clamp on wage-price and other production-allocating controls. No, says this adamant champion of the unhampered market economy; if interventionism is foolish in peacetime, it is doubly foolish in wartime when the nation's very survival is at stake. All the government has to do is to raise all the funds needed for the conduct of the war by taxing the citizens and by borrowing exclusively from them—not from the central or commercial banks. Because the money supply would not then be swollen and everybody would have to cut back his consumption drastically, inflation would not be a great problem. Public consumption, through a greatly augmented inflow of tax revenues and borrowed funds, would advance while private consumption would fall. The upshot would be the absence of inflation.

By the same token, Mises has no stomach for the idea that a nation could simply deficit-spend its way to prosperity, as advocated by many of Keynes's followers. He holds that such economic thinking is fallaciously based on governmental "contra-cyclical policy." This policy calls for budget surpluses in good times and budget deficits in bad times so as to maintain "effective demand" and hence "full employment."

But Mises regards the "G" in Keynes's "full employment" formula of $Y = C + I + G$; (National Income = Consumption Spending + Investment Spending + Government Spending) as about the most unstable, politics-ridden, and unscientific balancing wheel that the economic managers could employ. For one thing, the formula ignores the political propensity to spend, good times or bad. And for another, it ignores market-sensitive cost-price relationships and especially the proclivity of trade unions and minimum wages to price labor out of markets—i.e., into unemployment.

Thus he holds Keynesian theory, in practice, proceeds through fits of fiscal and monetary expansion and leads to inflation, controls, and ultimately stagnation. Further, "G," so used, generally means the secular swelling of the public sector and shrinking of the private sector—a trend that spells trouble for human liberty. In a way, he anticipated and rebutted the Keynesian thesis a quarter-century ahead of Keynes in his 1912 work, *The Theory of Money and Credit*, in which he contended that uneconomic wages and forced-draft credit expansion, and not capitalism *per se*, carried the seeds of boom and bust.

To be sure, many economists and businessmen have long felt that Mises is entirely too adamant, too unyielding. If that is a fault, he is certainly guilty. But Ludwig von Mises, the antithesis of sycophancy and expediency, the intellectual descendant of the Renaissance, believes in anything but moving with what he regards as the errors of the times. He has long sought the eternal verities. He believes in the dignity of the individual, in the sovereignty of the consumer, in the limitation of the state. He opposes the planned society, whatever its manifestation. He holds that a free society and a free market are inseparable. He glories in the potential of reason and man. In sum, he stands for principle in the finest tradition of Western Civilization. And from that rock of principle, during a long and fruitful life, this titan of our time has never budged.

Mises in America[1]

Gary Schlarbaum, I thank you for this award and high honor from your grand legacy in loving memory of a genius in our time, Ludwig von Mises (1881–1973). But let me say up front, fellow Misesians, meet me, Mr. Serendipity, Bill Peterson, here by a fluke, a child of fickle fate. For, frankly, I had never heard of the famous Mises when I took his course for its Monday night 8–10:00 slot neatly fitting my New York University schedule back in 1949.

Sure, night school's OK for me, an assistant economics prof at Brooklyn Polytech. But why for a genius like Mises? Why would no Ivy League university here nor prestigious university in Europe find a chair for him? Good question. Murray Rothbard gave three reasons: (1) Mises was a Jew when in the first half of the twentieth

---

[1]William H. Peterson is the winner of the 2005 Gary G. Schlarbaum Award for Lifetime Achievement in the Cause of Human Liberty, awarded annually by the Mises Institute. This is his acceptance speech, delivered October 8, 2005.

century anti-Semitism ran high; (2) Mises was a laissez-fairest—for government *de minimus* to protect person and property only; and (3) Mises was a noncompromiser, a Rock of Gibraltar who would not yield to politically correct Keynesianism, Marxism, Welfarism, funny money, or state hegemony.

But what of academic freedom? Even NYU, in offering Mises a "visiting professorship"—he so visited for 24 years—offered no pay. It had to be raised outside. For shame, you lords of Academe here and abroad.

Yet for me happenstance became circumstance, and I soon met like-minded fellow students like Murray Rothbard, George Reisman, Israel Kirzner, Hans Sennholz, Ralph Raico, and Louis Spadaro who, with Mises as a catalyst, made names for themselves in Austrian literature. So synergy blossomed on Washington Square.

But let Mr. Serendipity add proudly: Lu became my mentor, a dear friend and colleague at NYU from 1949 on, until the world lost him in 1973. But not forever—thanks to his sweeping ideas and to this lively working memorial, the Ludwig von Mises Institute, the think tank that keys human action, that sees history as anything but predetermined, that puts to America Hamlet's fateful question, explored here: To be or not to be?

That question bears on the Mises Institute's basic *raison d'être* and *modus operandi*, and, in a telling way, on Gertrude Stein's deathbed words to her close friend Alice B. Toklas. For, as she lay dying in Paris in 1946, she asked, "What is the answer?" Alice shrugged. "Well then," Gertrude pressed on, "what is the question?" Misesians, isn't there a lesson here for us? Isn't our job in big part to reject and refute status quo answers piled on us daily, and instead question, question, question the coercive powers that be? Well, Misesians—contrarians for now, libertarians forever—have you wondered how the Mises Institute came to be?

Some history is in order. . . .

First, let me note how well I remember Lu Mises and his dear wife, Margit. Margit often came with him to class. And, after studying typing and stenography at a Manhattan secretarial school, this glamorous star of the Berlin and Vienna stage came to type every page—and even retype quite a few—in her quite green language of English, of all 900 pages of the Mises *magnum opus*, *Human Action* (1949). I ask you: Isn't such human action truly a labor of love? The more so with Lu's firm rule (ahem) of having Margit correct a typo by retyping the entire page?

Hail then Margit Mises, a giant in her own right. It was visionary Margit who approved the founding of the Mises Institute in 1981, with that mission accomplished in 1982. Backing the project were other giants such as F.A. Hayek, Lawrence

Fertig, Henry Hazlitt, and Murray Rothbard, who led academic programs here until his death in 1995. Think-tank execs of the caliber of Lew Rockwell, Pat Barnett, and Jeff Tucker closed the deal to put this great think tank of hope and root reform on the intellectual front. Look around this room. See scores of supporters who have bet on Mises, on seeing his world of freedom and free enterprise aglimmering. Misesians, take heart. And. . . .

Let's celebrate the prodigious life of Lu Mises, a life in which he fused crowning insight on how the world tackles the law of scarcity with lifelong moral courage. He showed that courage in class as a great teacher—I was there—and in academic debate as a great fighter, as Margit tells in her book *My Years with Ludwig von Mises*. He was also, as F.A. Hayek, his Nobel Prize-winning student, noted, "a great radical, an intelligent and rational radical . . . a radical on the right lines." Mises a radical, a nonconformist? Yes, as were Aristotle, Newton, Galileo, Adam Smith, and Einstein in their own nonconforming day.

Mises revealed a source of that moral courage in *Notes and Recollections*[2], a somber book he did in 1940 after he and Margit narrowly

---

[2]A new translation by Arlene Oost-Zinner is now available entitled *Memoirs* (Auburn, Ala.: Ludwig von Mises Institute, 2009).

escaped Nazi Europe and landed in New York. In the book, Lu cited a Latin verse by Virgil which he had adopted as a young man. As the verse translates into English: "Do not yield to evil but always oppose it with courage." The motto served him well, for all his much-challenged life.

In this light of such courage—yours as well as his—let's discuss some of his big ideas, dwelling on one, to me, very hopeful idea: Lu's widening the definition and application of an overworked and much misunderstood word, democracy. Democracy is, I say, commonly but wrongly equated with freedom, as shown in history, as I will cite.

Yet in the Mises sense of the word, it does equate with freedom beautifully, effectively— getting, for example, not a biennial 50 percent but a 100 percent daily election turnout of Americans and other Westerners. Call it direct democracy, market democracy, above all, voluntary democracy. So why don't we call it as it is, America's True Democracy? I'll get back to it.

Meanwhile, Misesians, let's salute Lu Mises, the dean, the master builder of Austrian economics in the twentieth century—as was Carl Menger in the nineteenth. Menger, it is well said, founded the Austrian School in 1871 on the intellectual bedrock of subjectivism and marginal utility as keys to value.

Subjectivism and marginal utility? And how, Misesians. For the central idea of Mises, as I view him, lies in his extending this concept into the very title and theme of *Human Action*, as well as into his entire economic scheme of things. For, here, Mises caught the role of the acting individual, so missing in mainstream economics, so utterly *persona non grata* in mathematical economics; that is, Mises saw the individual mind, individual spirit, individual personality together as the prime mover in economic theory and practice.

That is, Mises put individualism and the individual—you, for example—back in the economic picture, in and out of the market; Mises ruled out as human action reflexive or unconscious action such as breathing, sweating, sleeping, aging, and so on.

Thus, what Mises forged intellectually is "praxeology," the vision that purposeful human action, including division of labor, is central to society, social cooperation, human survival—to Western Civilization itself. So, fellow praxeologists, Lu saw human action spring from thinking into individually directed behavior—for example, your own.

Consider this analogy, if you will: Descartes held in 1637: "I think, therefore I am." Held Mises, as I see him: "I think, therefore I act." So thought begets action. Human action is acting consciously, goaded by gain, sometimes after a snap judgment, sometimes after deliberation—from scratching your nose, to getting married, to changing careers, to rethinking economics along Austrian lines. By the way, if every human action hinges on gain, pecuniary or nonpecuniary, doesn't that make every so-called nonprofit organization a contradiction in terms? You bet.

Critically, too, Mises saw the market not as a place, but as a process, a dynamic process of social cooperation in which the dual-roled, consumer-producer individual—such as you—chooses his/her division-of-labor partners directly/indirectly, in a grand, peaceful, choiceful, constructive, spontaneous order. We tag this order variously: community, business, commerce, society. I suspect that, if he had to, Mises might cut economics to one word: *choosing* or its derivative, *choices*. Recall, Lu himself also called them votes.

Misesians, see then how human action, i.e., conscious choosing or voting in or out of the market, can affect the teaching of, say, Gresham's Law. College kids in Economics 101 learn the law as "bad money drives good money out of circulation." True, as far as it goes. Yet such teaching shortchanges the student who should be told of the human action involved: how holders of irredeemable paper money consciously choose to put it back into circulation, so choosing to hold on to their good money such as gold or gold certificates. Or, how such teaching affects the learning of Say's Law as "supply creates demand." True again (in a macro sense), but without the Mises idea of human action, students are unlikely to see why capitalists and entrepreneurs focus so hard on prices, competition, technology, marketing, productivity, etc.—as ordered by you and other sovereign consumers.

Hear then how Mises put such key ideas of consumer sovereignty and market democracy in *Human Action*. Hear his style as well as substance:

> The direction of all economic affairs is in the market society a task of the entrepreneurs. Theirs is the control of production. They are at the helm and steer the ship. A superficial observer would believe that they are supreme. But they are not. They are bound to obey unconditionally the captain's orders. *The captain is the consumer.* [Emphasis mine] Neither entrepreneurs nor the farmers nor the capitalists determine what has to be produced. The consumers do that. If a businessman does not strictly obey the orders of the public as they are conveyed to him by the structure of market prices, he suffers losses, he goes bankrupt, and is thus removed from his eminent position at the helm. Other men who did better in satisfying the demand of consumers replace him. (p. 270)

Vintage Mises, praxeologists, but how come in recent years much of America has embraced neo-conservatism throughout the land? A neo-con, famously said its godfather, Irving Kristol, "is a liberal who has been mugged by reality." Yet Kristol, author of *Two Cheers for Capitalism* (1978) should still be asked: Why but two and not three cheers for capitalism? Doesn't this show a bias for state hegemony over business? Or, to plumb another famous Kristol line: "Democracy does not guarantee equality of conditions; it only guarantees equality of opportunity." Yet doesn't even this guarantee imply opportunities for clever government meddlers to fiddle with the starting, if not the finishing, line of society?

So no wonder the "Bring 'Em On," neo-conned and neo-conning White House worships the demigod of political democracy via our media, textbooks, legislatures, even echoing the 1917 World War I motto of "Make the World Safe for Democracy" to a bemused globe? Democracy? Misesians, I ask you: To what end? My answer lies in the words of Benjamin Disraeli, then a young novelist, sharp thinker, and back-bench Tory M.P. (later twice becoming Britain's Prime Minister) in the House of Commons on March 31, 1850. Listen and wonder if you're hearing a recitation on America in 2005:

> If you establish a democracy, you must in due time reap the fruits of democracy. You will in due season have great impatience of the public burdens, combined in due

season with great increase of public expen-
diture. You will in due season have wars
entered into from passion and not from
reason; and you will in due season submit
to peace ignominiously sought and ignominiously obtained, which will diminish
your authority and perhaps endanger your
independence.

Or, Misesians, hear the corroborative editorial on democracy's venal consort of politics in
The London Times not long after, on February 7,
1852. Listen:

Concealment, evasion, factious combina-
tions, the surrender of convictions to party
objects, and the systematic pursuit of
expediency are things of daily occurrence
among men of the highest character, once
embarked in the contentions of political
life.

". . . contentions of political life"? Ah, that
consort and curse of politics: timeless, ubiqui-
tous politics, the contagious corrupter of political democracy and its minions from Ancient
Greece to America today, as implied in the title
of University of Nevada Las Vegas economist
and Mises Institute Distinguished Scholar Hans-
Herman Hoppe's book of 2001: *Democracy—The
God That Failed*. Or as implied by Hamlet stand-
ing in a Danish graveyard at night, holding up a

skull, and wondering if it had once belonged to a politician whom he identified as "one who would circumvent God."

So let's seek today's political import of Disraeli's prescience and that *London Times* editorial, noting how akin were some earlier thinkers on democracy. Take Plato, for example, citing democracy in his *The Republic* (c. 370 B.C.) as "a charming form of government, full of variety and disorder, and dispensing a kind of equality to equals and unequals alike." Or, Aristotle in his *Rhetoric* (c. 322 B.C.) blaming democracy in that it "when put to the strain, grows weak, and is supplanted by oligarchy." As did later thinker George Bernard Shaw, hitting democracy for opting "election by the incompetent many for appointment by the corrupt few." Or H.L. Mencken famously defining an election as "an advance auction of stolen goods." (Pray, stolen from whom?)

Or, Miscsians, see how America's Founders themselves saw political democracy courting self-ruin for the way many voters join "factions" or special interests which cut into liberty. James Madison spoke for his peers in *Federalist Papers* No. 10 (1787), seeing democracies as, I quote,

> spectacles of turbulence and contention [which] have ever been found incompatible with personal security or the rights of property, and have in general been as short

in their lives as they have been violent in
their deaths.

No wonder the very word "democracy" is
not to be found in the entire Declaration of Independence, Constitution, or Bill of Rights. Indeed,
look how sternly anti-democratic are the first five
words of the First Amendment on bills abridging
religion, speech, press, assembly, and petition:
"*Congress shall pass no law* [my emphasis]...."
Or look how the Framers, fearful of democracy,
tied up our Constitution with checks and balances
from federalism (harmed by the Civil War, the
14th Amendment of 1868, and the 17th Amendment of 1913) to a stop against an income tax
(undone by the 16th Amendment in 1913). Ben
Franklin, asked what kind of state the Framers
provided, raised a classic proviso: "A republic,
if you can keep it." Big if. I think Old Ben was
warning us: As political democracy swells, the
individual shrinks.

Yet—*voila*—Lu Mises lit up a near unknown
yet much safer and surer democracy—a way out
of our definitional crisis, if you will. In 1922, in
his great book *Socialism*, he saw true democracy
at work in market action. See it yourself: voting from the shopping mall to online buying, to
getting colas from vending machines, to filling
up at the gas pump by credit card, to business

consumers ordering supplies for their operations, and so on.

So these and other market voters vote, not but every other year, but again and again every day. Freely. Directly. In a way, one on one, so you elect your supplier, you get what you order, you are in charge. Great. Yet look: You and I are still under an Ancient Roman edict to consumers of *caveat emptor*: Let the buyer beware. And let stockholders beware of corrupt leaders such as those heading Enron and WorldCom. But given the human condition, don't we see some inevitable flotsam in business, a tiny minority of wrongdoers, a few weak CEOs often caught and punished? So why the U.S. big gun of the Sarbanes-Oxley Act with its heavy oversight regulation becoming but more costly intervention, more drag on freedom and free enterprise, more burdens on the backs of consumers?

Yet Mises in *Socialism* gave market democracy a vital political edge today. If we use it. Misesians, hear and seek to put his brilliant edge, his near-law, into public opinion play:

> When we call a capitalist society a consumers' democracy, we mean that the power to dispose of the means of production, which belongs to the entrepreneurs and capitalists, can only be acquired by means of the consumers' ballot, held daily in the marketplace. (p. 21)

Mises was right, spending his life seeking limits on loudly trumpeted political democracy. Democracy. Check its Greek roots: rule or *kratia*, by the people, the demos. But also check how Big Government snares and deludes you today: For example, who really rules whom? How come state hegemony, heavy taxation, deficit finance, intervention galore, burgeoning bureaucracy, and sick, public-government schools—i.e., sick from four basic ills: (1) peddling moral relativism, (2) teacher unionization, (3) denial of competition, and (4) its kiss of death, denial of choice?

So ponder: Just how does political democracy cause the state to shine and the free individual to fade? Or how come inflation ever devalues fiat money across the globe in a seemingly endless form of legal larceny? In the U.S., M.D.s charged $2 for an office visit, $3 a home visit in 1930 when I was growing up in Jersey City, but now an office visit can cost $80 or more, when a first-class stamp cost two cents but now 37 cents, when a N.Y.C. subway ride cost a nickel but now $2, when I worked at the A&P for a minimum hourly wage of 25 cents (if today I find the idea of a minimum wage inane, as it disemploys the poor), when a man's haircut cost 25 cents but now I pay $20 or 80 times more at my barber? Or, why do winner-take-all elections split society ("us vs. them")? Or, why endless insurgency violence in

Iraq or suicide bombers in New York, Madrid, London, and elsewhere?

Three cheers then for the Mises perception of productive and most peaceful market democracy—and three boos for society's mortal enemy, the state unlimited. Did Mises say peaceful? Look, mindful of terrorists about: Doesn't capitalism/ social cooperation across borders say it's dumb to shoot your customers or bomb your investors, thereby harming your very own people? So in current debate on economic policy, I urge you to perceive and work for peaceful, productive, market democracy, which, if imperfect, could come to be rethought, reinforced, even reborn, as could, it follows, human liberty. Ask yourself: Why?

Well, call it self-power to the people—individual by individual—call it *laissez-faire* capitalism, call it in this so-called war on terrorism "World Peace Through World Trade," the wise line of IBM founder Thomas J. Watson in the interwar period of the '20s and '30s, call it the market way of the choosy-choosing sovereign individual. Or, why not just call it what it is, again, America's True Democracy?

Yet the rub of our time is the quiet, almost unknown, ideological clash of coercive political democracy vs. voluntary market democracy, the public embrace of Big Government, the confusion of many if not most citizens that our Welfare-Warfare State is on their side, the irony that the modern state, which can still serve a vital function in providing due process and enforcing private property rights, can and most often does get out of hand today to punish the forgotten consumers—thanks but no thanks to rampant state intervention. And not just today's but tomorrow's consumers as our unfunded national debt in the tens of trillions of dollars (a 2003 U.S. Treasury study had it at $44.2 trillion) mounts, so now we praxeologists can say: "Blessed are the children, for they shall inherit the national debt."

Catch 22 of our times is then the neglect of historians and other gatekeepers to police the police, to have us "patriots" yield to the tyranny of the status quo including vast state spending, to what Tony Blair of Britain and Bill Clinton of the U.S. cutely called our mixed system, not the sick mixed-up system it is, but "The Third Way," an optimum mix of socialism and capitalism. Optimum? Please, Messrs. Blair and Clinton, don't put us on.

So, Misesians, our bipartisan Welfare-Warfare State—with its pre-Hurricane Katrina, 2006, $2.5 trillion federal budget, its initial deficit at $333 billion, its politics, its blatant amorality (Bastiat's "legal plunder")—drags on, bloats, a Frankensteinian monster running amok. Why? In a word, vice.

Per Alexander Pope (1734): "Vice is a monster of so frightful mien/As to be hated, needs but to be seen/But seen too oft, familiar with her face/We first endure, then pity, then embrace." Mae West put such human frailty differently: "I began as Snow White but I drifted."

No wonder that in 1956, or 49 years ago, Mises felt pushed to publish a book, *The Anti-Capitalistic Mentality*. But today anti-capitalism is more rife than ever. Indeed, Nobel economist F.A. Hayek, Mises's pupil, felt a duty to publish, in 1988, or 32 years later, a book on the lines of *The Anti-Capitalistic Mentality*. Hayek's title was *The Fatal Conceit: The Errors of Socialism*.

Recall this was the same Hayek who wrote his bestselling *The Road to Serfdom* in 1944, as we half-serfs today tread that very same road, as new Dr. Panglosses rhapsodize that we live in the best of all possible worlds, as Social Security with IRAs becomes part of our new so-called Ownership Society—with its sticky, paternalistic, federal control, with that mounting unfunded government lien on your property and heirs in the here-and-now as well as in the hereafter. Oh, how clever are these neo-conned and neo-conning Compassionate Conservatives—so compassionate with other people's money.

Conservatives? Misesians, ask a conservative how come Hayek added a postscript, "Why I Am Not a Conservative," to his 1960 book *The Constitution of Liberty*. To Hayek, conservatism is simply too unprincipled, too catch-as-catch-can, too neo-conned, in today's word.

Our fix reminds me, Misesians, of that observation of Harvard philosopher George Santayana who remarked: "The world is a perpetual caricature of itself; at every moment it is the mockery and the contradiction of what it is pretending to be."

Pretending is indeed the Washington game. Pretend independence, for instance. Recall House Speaker Sam Rayburn's attributed standard greeting to new Democrat members of Congress, per: "Remember, to get along, go along." Or the like line of Will Rogers, saying: "There is no more independence in politics than there is in jail."

But, Misesians, what of our independence from the state? Let me reply: For to all state-buffeted Americans awaiting deliverance come Mises, Rothbard, and the rest of us Austrians. Austrian economists and supporters are people of insight and action, not devotees of blind fate.

I'm reminded of the story told by Margit Mises. Once watching her husband play tennis with a coach and seeing her Lu not going for all the balls within his reach, she called out: "Why don't you put a little more effort in the game?" He replied: "Why should I? The fate of the ball does not interest me."

What did interest Lu was the folly of political democracy in state interventionism, or piecemeal socialism, or realization of his phrase of "planned chaos," of the mirage that government official-dom can somehow make man's lot so much better off—selflessly, if not magically.

How? Simple. By meddling with you and society in myriad ways, all counterproductive—from affirmative action to Social Security, to Medicare-Medicaid, "affordable housing," per-sonal and corporate income taxes, gun control, the Food and Drug Administration, the Environ-mental Protection Agency, tort lawyers driving up malpractice insurance premiums so high as to drive many medical specialists out of business, to trying to stop the vile practice of "outsourc-ing" or "Exporting America," but of course not noting "insourcing," such as Toyota causing some 200,000 jobs to take root here.

So Mises saw state intervention ever doling out unintended results, ever boomeranging, ever making intended beneficiaries worse off in the long run.

Take affirmative action. Do we really make women better off by the government forcing employers to pay them equal pay for equal work? Sounds fair to many, but doesn't such gender inter-vention inhibit women from competing against men by, if need be, cutting their pay demands to win jobs and experience, or inhibit employers from favoring men over women without detection—unless the state resorts to quotas? As it often has.

Or take Prohibition, the "Noble Experiment" (1920–1933), the U.S. ban on production of alcoholic drink. It touched off a national epidemic of black markets and gangsters *à la* Legs Diamond and Lucky Luciano, making headlines with their street warfare. Luckily, if incongruously, Congress reversed its lax ways, permitting the 21st Amendment to repeal the 18th Amendment. But that repeal left intact the then nascent but now virulent War on Drugs with deadly implications for U.S. domestic policy today in terms of renewed street warfare and for foreign policy involving the U.S. in a war on drug traffic from Colombia to Afghanistan. But brilliant Lu would have had none of it. Hear him in *Human Action*:

> Opium and morphine are certainly dangerous habit-forming drugs. But once the principle is admitted that it is the duty of government to protect the individual against his own foolishness, no serious objections can be advanced against further encroachments. . . . Is not the harm a man can inflict on his mind and soul even more disastrous than any bodily evils? Why not prevent him from reading bad books and seeing bad plays. . . ? If one abolishes man's freedom to determine his own consumption, one takes all freedoms away. (pp. 728–29)

More Mises. Leonard Read, then top manager of the L.A. Chamber of Commerce, told the story of his guest speaker, Mises, who spoke in 1943 of the plight of the U.S. war effort with Washington slapping on wage and price controls, setting priorities or allocations of commodities, rationing gas and meat to consumers, allowing local authorities to install rent control, etc., or what Mises tagged "war socialism." After the talk, a member of the audience asked the speaker: "It is a depressing prospect you have outlined, Dr. Mises. Considering the program the politicians have adopted and its inevitable, terrible consequences, what would you do, if by chance, you were made dictator of this country. What first step would you take?" Mises's eyes lit up and quick as a flash, he replied with a grin, "I would abdicate."

Whither then in 2005 our berated, underrated, far over-regulated, and deeply misread capitalistic order? Yet isn't it still, per our Founders (though the word capitalism had yet to be coined), a royal road to social cooperation, a vast vital network of private governments of the people, by the people, for the people, all blessed with individual assent—highly-used switchable assent?

Switchable? And how. So see in our society countless private governments, such as Harvard, *New York Times*, New York Stock Exchange, Microsoft, Southern Baptists, Salvation Army, Wal-Mart, the Mises Institute, and some 30

million other private firms, farms and organiza-
tions of all varieties; yet all rely on switchable
individual assent. So you're free to switch from
Ford to Toyota, from Yale to MIT, from Wendy's
to McDonald's. And vice versa. Talk about true
private democracy.

Democracy? But isn't this our political
shield for a global *Pax Americana* to chastise a
sinful, quite undemocratic world, with the focus
now on the turbulent Middle East? And doesn't
this serve up de Juvenal's classic conundrum (74
A.D.): "But who is to guard the guards themselves?" Or, Misesians, note how Thomas Paine
saw government in his *Common Sense* (1776) as
"a necessary evil," on which Mises commented, a
government properly restrained wouldn't be evil.
Its only duty would be to seek to provide security
to person and property. So the Mises perception
of self-government waxes into individualistic
government based on self-ownership.

Still, Bismarck likened the legislative process
to the unsightly change of pigs into sausages. Or
said Churchill, democracy is the least awful way
to effect a peaceful change of political power.
Or, as Swiss thinker Felix Somary put it in his
Democracy at Bay (1952): Political democracy
blends two "fictions," one the idea that "an entire
people can assume sovereignty," and the other the
idea of "the innate goodness of man." Fictions?
Oh yes.

So, Misesians, let's juxtapose America's forceful Political Democracy with Lu's insight of voluntary Consumers/Market Democracy to see which is which and why. As I ask you: With both in need of reform, which needs the most drastic by far?

Look. In one democracy you vote but every other year for candidates (who may not win) to "represent" you and many others indirectly on myriad issues. In the other, you vote daily, often, directly, for specific vendors, goods, or services, an endless plebiscite going on every minute of every day, with dollars as ballots.

Yes, some get more ballots than others. Yet Mises saw this result as logical and moral as some are more productive than others. He also saw this outcome as often transient, as consumers vote "poor people rich and rich people poor," per his *Human Action*. Yes, one democracy is public, the other private. One veers socialistic and pro-state as it funds failing programs and public schools; the other veers capitalistic and pro-consumer as it lets failing firms and private schools fail. One is coercive and centralized, the other voluntary and decentralized.

One runs, inadvertently, a growth-impeding, win-lose, zero-sum game with neither a guiding market system nor economic calculation (to be spelled out in a minute); the other runs, also inad-vertently, a pro-growth, win-win, positive-sum game, with a guiding market system and economic calculation. Misesians, this difference alone sets America's future for better or worse, for richer or poorer.

One democracy runs by politics, monopoly, winner-take-all, much hoopla, unmindful of H.L. Mencken's line that democracy amounts to the "worship of jackals by jackasses," or of Henry David Thoreau's *Civil Disobedience* of 1849 when he saw "little virtue in the action of masses of men," voting as "a sort of gaming." The other runs a market society by cooperation and competition. One forgets the individual, per Yale's William Graham Sumner's "The Forgotten Man" lecture in 1883; the other focuses on him/her, if imperfectly per spam in your PC and junk mail in your mailbox.

Too, one democracy plays incumbency tricks: gerrymandering, logrolling, warmongering, free-lunch guises such as big federal "grants"—bribes in effect—to states and localities (est. $365 billion 2005); the other is ever cleansed by competition, cost-cutting, and demonstrated market deeds for choosy-choosing sovereign consumers. One democracy veers to a Machiavellian amoral short run—for example, resorting to credit expansion aimed at winning elections if courting inflation and recession. The other veers to moral contracts and the longer run.

One, with coercive power, yields to Acton's law that power tends to corrupt and absolute power corrupts absolutely, as seen in fratricidal partisanship edging into mutually assured destruction (MAD), or in what House Speaker Jim Wright called "mindless cannibalism," or in Frank Chodorov's view of Washington's work as "the rape of society," or in Harry Truman's truism that "if you ever need a friend in Washington, buy a dog," or in the no-brainer that the Welfare-Warfare State will wise up some day and swear off its misdeeds. Sure. Or, as Gertrude Stein said of Oakland, California, so we Austrians say of bankrupt state interventionism: "There is no there there."

Yet market democracy, Misesians, if gloriously voluntary, if the very wellspring of our well-being, if our escape route to sanity and safety, can and does slip into flotsamesque personal and corporate misdeeds such as money-grasping or getting into bed with political power to win subsidies, import quotas, and other mischief via special interests. All this despite President Dwight Eisenhower's 1961 farewell warning of a "military-industrial complex," of an unholy alliance of Big Government and Big Business. See how catching is the Washington disease of legal kleptocracy to all comers, high and low. Recall that a kleptomaniac is a fellow who helps himself because he can't help himself. The looters in New Orleans and Baghdad are not alone.

One democracy can glorify war, including class warfare, the other glorifies peaceful trade in a virtual global concordance on private property rights (if widely knocked as "globalization"). One entered World War I, naïvely, as "The War to End War" and, again, "Make the World Safe for Democracy," only to reap—how's this for a cast of characters?—Lenin and Stalin in Russia, Hitler in Germany, Mussolini in Italy, Franco in Spain, Tojo in Japan, Tito in Yugoslavia, Mao in China, Perón in Argentina, Castro in Cuba, Allende in Chile, Pol Pot in Cambodia, Chavez in Venezuela, Mugabe in Zimbabwe—almost all of whom played or play charade democracy to get and hold power, as have lesser imitators over the world. Now President Bush seeks democracy in the Middle East, if not the whole world, while counting Germany and Japan as post-World War II "wins" for democracy, but he is silent on outright failures such as North Korea, Bosnia, Somalia, Iran, and Haiti (this Clinton invasion was gamely tagged as "Operation Democracy").

One democracy rues income disparity and, like Robin Hood, blithely "transfers" wealth from the Haves to the Have-Nots, the other lifts all boats, including those of the poor. One denies itself key market feedback data or what Mises called that aforementioned market-driven "economic calculation." In 1920 he brilliantly saw its absence as the key in the certain failure of socialism, a thesis he expanded in his 1922 book *Socialism*. Witness, then, in the second half of the twentieth century socialism collapse or misfire in the USSR, Eastern Europe, China, and in state welfare and other interventions everywhere. Witness American interventionism in spades. For its part, market democracy uses market figures such as prices and profit-and-loss to move scarce resources to their perceived highest-yielding uses.

Hear Mises in his 1944 classic *Bureaucracy*: "There are two methods for the conduct of human affairs within the frame of human society. One is bureaucratic management, the other is profit management." Misesians, note how bureaucratic management, denied market prices and economic calculation, flies blind. So it saps capital and talent (human capital) in a vast tragedy of the commons as special interests horn in on each other to grab all they can, while profit management saves and invests capital, the very fuel of economic growth.

Yes, self-interestedly. Yet, with private property rights, it does so creatively, spontaneously, harmoniously, constructively. Hayek called this remarkable self-guiding market process of economization-productivity-economic growth a "marvel."

So, Misesians, see how market democracy explains the success of the West, how Adam Smith's vivid metaphor for self-interest as the "invisible hand" fits into his system of "natural liberty," of winning self-help by helping others. Recall a famed line in his *The Wealth of Nations*: "It is not from the benevolence of the butcher, or the brewer, or the baker that we expect our dinner, but from their regard of their own interest." No question then that capitalism—Lu's politically-wise idea of market democracy—is America's true democracy, that its opposite: the bipartisan Welfare-Warfare State via coercive winner-take-all "democracy," is a case of planned chaos, of a nation chasing its tail or an end-of-rainbow pot-of-gold. Or, to quote Chicago School economist Herbert Stein's hopeful "law": "If something can't go on forever, it will stop." Not bad.

Or, if I may transform Lu into a modern-day Moses pleading with Egypt's Pharaoh, meaning today's myopic statists: Let my people [the consumers] go!

Three challenges remain, as I see it: First is need of steady insight. Or, in Lu's words: "The issue is always the same: the government or the market. There is no third solution."

The second challenge is: How can we use market democracy and other means to help tame political democracy as our Founding Fathers did in 1776, or will we willy-nilly let it slowly but surely snuff our civilization, our future, our very well-being?

And the third challenge is the need for tying the free market idea to a moral code based on virtue, honor, dignity, and wisdom, or on the Ten Commandments, which, by the way, is depicted on the Mises Institute seal. Yes, the free market is super, as real an ideal as we'll ever see, yet given human imperfection, it's no Nirvana. Or, as has been said for healthy living, Misesians: Eat well, stay fit, die anyway.

These challenges are made tougher by brainy if adaptable economists like Fritz Machlup, a Mises student who won prestigious university chairs and indeed the presidency of the American Economic Association. Why then did Mises have a three-year falling-out with Fritz? I was, in a way, in the middle of it. Fritz and his wife Mitzi were our friends and neighbors in Princeton where we lived while Mary and I remained of course close to Lu and Margit Mises in New York. I heard both sides.

Imagine, the rift was over gold.

Hear Fritz in a paper he gave at Rockford College in 1971 on his rift with his mentor. Hear its Keynesian overtones: "As long as governments, politicians, and voters believe that monetary policy should be used to secure more employment or faster growth, it is not feasible to maintain fixed exchange rates or a fixed price of gold." Not feasible? But of course, Fritz.

So Machlup turns out to be a successful pragmatist, Mises—what else?—a lifelong classical liberal, an indomitable genius, ever a liberator. First, good news: Thanks to Margit reaching Lu, the tiff ended. And Fritz was helpful in getting the American Economic Association to name Lu as Distinguished Fellow. The bad news: Keynesianism and political democracy bloat on—the Nanny State, or by Austrian lights, America's Magnificent Failure: Wherein Worshipped Government Itself Is the Problem, Not the Solution.

All this, as Lu's market democracy remains largely unappreciated, unloved, unexplained, even much unexploited, so harming society. But for how long? Ah, back to that Hamlet-like question for America: To be or not to be? Yet recall what follows right on in Hamlet's soliloquy is yet another big question:

> Whether 'tis nobler in the mind to suffer/
> The slings and arrows of outrageous for-
> tune/Or, to take arms against a sea of trou-
> bles/And by opposing end them?

Let me tackle both questions: First, Misesians, Let us be. Meaning: You—alive, active, able, alert. And, second, let us intellectually oppose the hypocrisy and expediency of an increasingly unlimited, adversarial, anti-consumer

Leviathan. Yet doesn't Leviathan itself boil down to One Big Bad Idea? Recall, Misesians, per dear Lu, ideas rule the world and ideas change.

So I enlist each and every one of you to personally scour and plug Austrian ideas, to stay tuned, stay strategic, stay innovative, stay responsive, stay responsible, stay entrepreneurial, stay optimistic, stay resolute, stay profitable, increasingly so, if you can, so to serve society all the more. And, stay strong and true for the Ludwig von Mises Institute, its people, its programs and, above all, its ideas. Bear in mind, ideas have consequences, good and bad. Misesians, fight then the good fight. Thank you, my dear fellow Misesians.

Sharpening the Student Mind—and Yours: The Second Mile[1]

"What Makes Sammy Run?" I quote the title of a once best-selling novel. With the point today, Teachers-Students-Others: What makes you run? Run for your respective teaching-learning-other duties (whoever you are), but, especially, your thinking?

Thinking, Teachers-Students-Others, has clicked for us, yes. Note one indicator: Public applications for admission to our charter school, the Franklin Academy, Wake Forest, North Carolina, run some 1,000 over some 100 available annual openings, a 10–1 ratio. Q.E.D. Still, best ask:

---

[1]An expansion of remarks to Luddy School teachers and students delivered at the Annual Conference, Raleigh, N.C., November 13–14, 2008.

What now for an encore, a finesse, a boost? How can we get each of us to dig deeper into our respective reasoning reserve and come up with a still sharper mind?

In other words, how can we spur ourselves so to analyze each one's personal teaching-learning-other circumstances by, as a starter, continually asking of relevant current and past events a simple, "Why?"

Or, baldly, how can we get more bang for the buck?

I say, go The Second Mile: Make your thinking, Teacher-Student-Other more logical, accessible, productive, appreciated. Best then that each of them and each of us be reminded: Your mind matters, so think smarter, go for it.

Overall, easier said than done. Yet, Fellow Human Beings, Fellow Teachers, Fellow Students, are not we all, broadly speaking, lifetime teachers, lifetime students, so lifetime communicators, lifetime motivators, each of us an activator-accelerator of the human mind—your own first and foremost—and others in and out of your subject (mine is economics)?

Thus, Fellow Mind Motivators, note our dual calling—in content and in context.

Context, the broad environment of the mind, challenges us: For our theme today sets a search for a possible self-renaissance of your mind, of escalating it to a higher plateau.

Modesty may be needed here. I'm reminded of the boast of Oscar Wilde arriving at U.S. customs in 1882 for a declaration, and saying: "I have nothing to declare except my genius."

For just what ways and means can we marshal to spur ourselves to learn to think sharper still?

Let me then spot Spur No. One of ten overlapping mind spurs covered here as that of a *Self-Thinker*, a key role, a self-aimer at a mind focused, concerned, involved—anything but scattered.

So our mission here is to seek to prod our respective mind-expansion and mind-creativity activities, so to lift each one's overall alertness, ability, person-career progress, and sense of general wellbeing and satisfaction. Key question is: Prod how?

Well, at work—you young and not-so-young Self-Thinkers—is your own self-directed mind busily mapping a dynamically varying future, individual by individual, circumstance by circumstance. Thus do contextual challenges emerge. How come?

Because, fact, you and I each live in and through a highly-individualized, highly-circumstanced mind.

Because, fact, Teachers-Students-Dear Readers, with your guidance and encouragement, including unshakeable self-encouragement, you can apply these thinking tools, these ten mind spurs, to a goal of enhancing-harnessing ongoing self-development, self-discovery, self-creativity. Call it harnessing success.

Because, fact, Teacher-Student-Reader, cannot you reinvigorate-redirect your mind to better face and beat circumstances, solve problems, and hone sharper thinking skills? I say: Why not?

Because, fact, Self-Thinkers, when you think about it, are we not each blessed with a working, introspective, evolving mindset, one that helps explain, as perceived, passing events in class, homework, elsewhere, including local and world events such as a worldwide economic recession involving world unemployment.

Because, fact, each can-do mindset can be broadened and deepened, sifting such events and fresh suppositions through an objective-moral framework, again starting by their asking an easy occasional "Why this?" or "Why that?"

As you, Dear Readers and Luddy School Teachers-Students often follow up such self-queries via checking an encyclopedia or Googling for answers.

So let's praise the inquisitive teacher/student/ whomever, one whose mind becomes a stepping-stone to greater person-career-potentiality— which sets a wider range of life possibilities than does the narrower, simpler idea of "potential."

For the message of potentiality—a second factor in the broad environment of the mind—is: You are likely a deeper thinker, a bigger person, than you think you are. The further message is: Put introspection to work, find that inner person spelling future success.

So, Dear Reader, enjoy a likelihood of perceiving success in class, home, office, lodge, event, church—wherever—thanks to your at least hoped-for, first-rate self-thinking throughout youth and adulthood. So capitalize on your person-career possibilities, create human capital, and win fame and maybe fortune.

Which reminds me of the title of another best-seller, this one by renowned mind motivator of a few decades ago, Napoleon Hill, *Think and Grow Rich*.

For, Fellow Teachers, Fellow Students, Fellow Readers, are we not all in the mind business so to better invest our time and talent to fulfill a highly personalized-highly individualized future?

The future is it. How to optimize that future, mind by mind, individual by individual, circumstance by circumstance, meaning you personally, is our goal here and now. Optimization may call for understanding a certain dichotomy of quite a few fellow human beings, to invoke again Oscar Wilde, who said: "Some cause happiness wherever they go; others, whenever they go."

Look. Grasping-knowing your own mind is central to self-development, a self-renaissance. Recall, Dear Readers-Fellow Teachers-Fellow Students, the thought of René Descartes who said in 1637: "I think, therefore I am."

Tie that idea to that of my unequaled NYU economist-mentor Ludwig von Mises with his great contribution to our teaching-learning job. See it in his sharply-titled major opus, *Human Action*, in 1949 when he said in effect: "I think, therefore I act."

So mind-action commits you to act individualistically, or by what Mises described as "methodological individualism."

Individualism explains my strict use of "self" to qualify each of these ten spurs to sharpen thinking. That self is the sovereign you—king or queen of your mind and will, of consequent individual actions, as each life continues to unfold better via your sharper self-interest, self-direction, self-thinking.

Self-thinking thus precedes and directs action in both teaching and learning. I ask you: Does not self-thinking link cause and effect, repeat cause and effect? So, on to Mind Spur No. 2: Be a *Self-Causationist*.

Causationist is an idea of Ralph Waldo Emerson. He held the solid self-thinker ties the cause to the effect in multifaceted life-knowledge-history, again as perceived, so lending a causationist bent to each mind, each age, each teacher, each student, each person—no matter who you are.

Style may help. For, say, on pointing up how the law of gravity works, a science teacher could add a light touch, saying: "Students, now don't let gravity get you down."

So I pass along this teaching-learning thought-action mindset of the Self-Causationist, of asking oneself not just why something happens, but raising more pointed questions:

What and Why Is a Gerrymander in American History? or, How Does the World Earn Its Living? or, What Is the Right Role of the State, the Family, Private Property? or, Why Inflation, or Why Our Painful Seesaw Business Cycle? or, Why Did Lincoln's Emancipation Proclamation Stop Short of Such Slave-Holding States as Maryland and West Virginia, or What Makes Man Tick?

Or, for our students asking: Just Who Am I? or, How Can I Become More Person-Career-Capable? or, How Does Each Luddy School Course Tie In with the Others? Why Is Deportment As Valuable As Academic Subjects? And so on.

So hail again the searching reflective mind, teacher by teacher, student by student, person by person (again whoever you are). So laud the entrepreneurial or venturesome mind, on its way to greater person-career-potentiality, to, I say, likely adult fame and maybe fortune.

Readers-Teachers-Students, let me then commend this Emersonian cause-effect spur to your TLC.

Now, background on these ten mind spurs, those loaded opening questions on why Sammy, you and I run. No surprise, it's self-interest, and so this a how-to overview of how to put it into play more effectively.

Ponder. Your mind awake directly/indirectly targets on and so reflects self-interest, meaning self-survival, self-direction—if imperfectly.

Imperfect was Saint Augustine before sainthood when he asserted uninhibited self-interest and beseeched Heaven: "Give me chastity and continence, but not yet."

True, that was a strained self-interest, Dear Reader, perhaps explaining its so-so reputation by many today who misjudge it as but naked greed or selfishness, even if such stances can and do occur. Often.

I ask: Was it not better judged in Adam Smith's 1776 classic work, *The Wealth of Nations*? There classical economist Smith, professor of moral philosophy at the University of Glasgow, drew a shrewd metaphor for universal constructive moral self-interest.

It was and is an Invisible Hand, a social helping hand, as witness this line in Smith's major opus: "It is not from the benevolence of the butcher, the brewer, or the baker that we expect our dinner, but from their regard for their own interest."

For what makes you and me run faster, farther, is universal-moral-constructive-peaceful self-interest spurred, I submit, by applied sharper self-thinking, aided-abetted by our ten spurs here.

So see self-interest, Dear Reader, as so infusive-suffusive that it prevails in every waking moment in each of us, directing your every move, every action—I say your very soul. For you, God-like, run you.

But not carte blanche, not wide-openly, not immorally. Indeed, does not each of us mostly come with a moral compass, with a personal vision, with often in the case of our students a cheerleader-coach—say, a caring teacher, mother or friend? And so all three ideas spark individual spirit and outlook.

Thus note: Each of us has a lifetime-job managing and upgrading our respective self-interest. Recall how each of us runs a unique DNA person—meaning nobody but nobody matches you ever in individuality and singularity. Think. You are one of a kind. But shouldn't you, in your own self-interest, direct and groom that one for higher things? And how!

So by applying the ten mind spurs noted here, superior person-career-potentiality ensues. Or so I hold and think you agree.

For, note, each of us has a self-monopoly, a self-sovereignty over oneself—again king or queen directing each one's mind and resulting actions.

But ensue contextual self-queries almost daily, per: Who, what, where, when, and how? Again, you decide, you implement wishes and ideas that can become reality, that can fulfill a dream—your own. Yes, various stretches between from contemplation to fulfillment take effort, time, sometimes worry, sometimes sweat. Still, it's your life, your call, and more power to you.

Illustratively, if atypically, I recall how brothers Wilbur and Orville Wright, running a bicycle shop in Dayton, Ohio, somehow transformed themselves into designers of a heavier-than-air aircraft that successfully took flight at Kitty Hawk, North Carolina in 1903, wowing the world, a tribute to freedom and free enterprise, to the fantastic power of the human mind.

Remember each of us has been given gifts of at least latent self-control, self-direction, self-discovery. Now if these gifts are in fact latent, why not activate them? Remember again you run you. You're in charge. It's your mind. It's your life. It's your future.

So each of us is mind-spurred by being a *Self-Constitutionalist*, a holder of an inner map of self-direction, an owner of a personal store of skills-values-morals, one saying just how we each cope—again thinkingly—with life's endless demands and exigencies.

So as we get to run our own mind, thus running each thought, each action, do we not do so as constituted, via each one's very own self-constitution, one amendable if not perfectible?

For, look, you and I can and do amend it, so usually spurring our respective overall thinking-acting deeds, if self-interestedly.

Why? Well, by so advancing mind control-personal vision, do we not also go far to ensure person-career success, intellectual growth, personal happiness as gains from respective upgraded self-interest? You bet!

Ah, pivotal self-interest again. Let's review it more closely. I say it runs you. It runs manufacturer and school director-supporter Bob Luddy and his wife Maria. It runs St. Thomas More Academy Headmaster Larry Henson and his wife Christy. It runs me and my wife Mary. It runs ex-President and First Lady Bush. It runs President Barack Obama and First Lady Michelle Obama, Secretary of State Hillary Clinton—and countless others.

In fact, it runs everybody the whole world over. Including the terrorist hell-bent on destroying infidels like you, Dear Reader.

So self-interest runs the housed, the homeless, the smart, the dumb, the doer, the lazy, the honest citizen, the outright criminal, including that aforementioned terrorist.

Criminal? A warped, anti-social mind? Sorry, yes. Man is often frail, flawed; criminality sets in.

So, Dear Reader, each viable, self-interested person such as you needs such guides as good sense, self-responsibility, reflection, commitment, the Ten Commandments—which are not, by the way, Ten Suggestions.

So should not you follow the moral imperative of Enlightened Self-Interest, of doing unto others what you would have others do unto you? No question.

So, Teachers-Students-Others, if not there now, why not add this life-force of Enlightened Self-Interest to your daily operations or, Teachers, to your lesson plan and class conduct, or, Students, to your learning diligence in and out of class? So see Enlightened Self-Interest enable each of us to take off anew—each with a sharper mind, with superior person-career potentiality on the move. Onward and upward, I say.

Back to those ten mind spurs, as I ask: Why not also build your sense of being a *Self-Envisioner*, a futurist regularly peering into a cloudy crystal ball on such matters as, if a student, college and career, or no matter who you are, tying together self-ownership- self-responsibility-self-direction? Direction? Forward march.

See then the Self-Envisioner's future already forming. Implicitly. So shouldn't that individual be told that his/her particular present-future bond impacts on self-growth in two vital ways?

First: Tell the Self-Envisioner that past is prologue, that future success involves success here and now.

Second: Tell the Self-Envisioner that a cumulative success system lies within, that it awaits activation by each futurist, that good action today inspires better action tomorrow, that success becomes a habit, that it awakens or reinforces self-esteem and self-initiative.

Regarding self-initative: Hear the advice by the father of TV star Sam Levinson who declares he's leaving the Brooklyn household to go on his own. Said his wise father: "Sam, remember if you ever need a helping hand, there's first one at the end of your arm."

So, Fellow Teachers-Fellow Students-Dear Readers, coax sharper minds, mind by mind, build brainpower one by one: So each of you should hit the books, concentrate, reflect, study thinkingly, tie as far as feasible past, present and future—all aiming to give you a head-start now and out ahead.

So tell Faculty-Students-Dear Readers, that good performance today is for one's own good, glory, gain—short-term, long-term.

Tell them: *Joie de vivre*: Enjoy life, smile, laugh, jest, see life's light zestful side as well as its other—so ducking stress, so accepting the medically-accepted fact that laughter is splendid medicine. (And costless medicine at that!)

Tell them as each of us optimizes opportunities, it is best to do so by serving others—so lifting their happiness as well as our own. Agreed that perspective takes self-vision, self-courage, self-thinking.

Tell them then of giant St. Thomas More, of his wit and grit in climbing the scaffold to be beheaded on order of Henry VIII, as More smiled and said: "See me safe up. For my coming down, I can shift for myself."

Another mind spur: Become a *Self-Competitor*, a self-runner, a self-discipliner, so to compete with oneself through self-scoring-self-tracking as well as competing with others such as fellow teachers or fellow classmates in your or other schools.

For, Teachers-Students, Readers, doesn't your optimizing self-interested opportunities play a key role in an ongoing social drama: Namely, your becoming more of an asset in the faculty, or in the student body, or in the family, or in the lodge, or in the company, or in your ongoing person-career-potentiality build-up, or more? Yes, indeed.

So, Teacher-Student-Dear Reader, observe ours is a highly competitive nation and globe, that the prizes go to prepared minds, to competition-tuned thinker-players everywhere. Emerson again, 1850: "Each child of the Saxon race is schooled to wish to be first." Or dig the 2008 Beijing Olympics lesson: Being first wins the gold.

Yet another of our ten teaching-learning spurs comes via an old Chinese adage: Fool me once, shame on you; fool me twice, shame on me. So our teaching-learning goal here is to stop such self-shame, cut self-delusion, profit from self-mistakes.

So, Dear Readers, why not adopt the mind spur in being a *Self-Realizer*, one who handles sometimes rough reality, one who, like the rest of us stumbles on occasion, but gets up, dusts one-self off, and starts all over again? Confucius has a tip here, saying c. 500 B.C., "Do not be ashamed of mistakes—and so make them crimes."

Yes, mistakes teach, valuably telling us what not to do. Teacher, student, parent—our key Luddy team—learn by them.

Yet another teaching-learning spur is in enriching one's treasury of words. Words are the building-blocks of the mind, the very means of creating thought, pursuing ends, attaining reason, gaining stature.

Thus: A strong case for you, Dear Reader, to become a *Self-Lexiconist*, a wordsmith, a possessor of a growing, working vocabulary. So keep that dictionary handy.

I recall a friendship with the William F. Buckley Jr., publisher and ace lexiconist of *National Review* who early on published my articles and had Mary and me visit his home in Sharon, Connecticut. He was the young author of *God and Man at Yale*. . . . His vocabulary? Awesome, ditto his diction and delivery.

Buckley once ran for mayor of New York City—famously saying he would demand a recount if he won. He wrote 50 books including novels, starred in the long-running weekly *Firing Line* TV show, gave speeches in the thousands, at the rate of about 70 a year for some 50 years. He was also a harpsichordist, a yachtsman—what a man!

The case of top public speaker-public writer Buckley suggests then a fresh thinking spur for us: Be a *Self-Expressionist*. For isn't thinking but expressing thoughts inwardly, while to write up or speak out is expressing your thoughts, your mind, outwardly to others?

So flew the flag of top Public Speaker-Public Writer Buckley who spoke out and wrote eloquently, historically (e.g., on the Cold War though he overdid it), his mind flashing in sound and print.

See then public speaking-public writing roles as spurs for self-growth, for gaining attention, for two maybe new roads to your sharper mind, to a greater person-career-potentiality build-up.

Think also of the mind spur in being an ace *Self-Chooser*, a realization that the good life amounts to regularly making smart choices, taking a cue from Shakespeare not to waste time, saying in *The Taming of the Shrew*: "There's small choice in rotten apples."

To be sure, the range of choices is broad—from just daily choices about what to wear or what to eat or what to do with open time, to bigger options such as friends, life-styles, character, mission, religion—of life's purpose.

Realize, Teachers-Students-Dear Readers, that thinking smarter is fruitful, satisfying, lasting, that the quality of life swings on the quality of individual choices, of ongoing, rising, individual repute.

Thus you grow smarter by thinking smarter, so making smarter choices, mostly lesser ones such as, say, what topic in an English creative-writing course, some critical, as choosing a marriage partner or a career in, say, medicine.

Yet just how does one reach this big choice or that? I say: Review ends, ideals, values, ethics. Counsel with family, friends, advisers, great thinkers of the past. Above all . . .

Think. But strategically, not casually. Know that to think is to choose, that to choose is to think. Thus do you gain by this teaching-learning spur aiming at smarter choices.

So tell yourself to choose well via Jefferson's Pursuit of Happiness, choice by choice, as you keep defining and refining yourself—as each of you becomes an ongoing work of self-progress, self-creativity, self-direction.

Last mind spur, frankly my favorite, is No. 10, that of being a *Self-Author*, a self-exceptionalist, a self-doer, a self-builder, a self-master, a self-controller, one who takes control over mind-body-purpose, one who, in effect, writes his/her own autobiography line by line, page by page, chapter by chapter, aiming and seeking a better beginning, a stronger middle, a happier ending. Again, it's your life, live it, direct it, rule it, enjoy it, write it—again not literally but not necessarily—as you move onward and upward, as I know you will.

So the sharp Self-Author puts into play the thought of a Greek head of state, Solon, saying "Know thyself" (c. 600 B.C.), or Aeschylus stating "God lends a helping hand to the man who tries hard" (c. 490 B.C.). Self-Author, self-exceptionalists, see and live up to the powerful point in *Invictus* (1888) by W.E. Henley:

It matters not how strait the gate,
How charged with punishments the scroll,

I am the master of my fate;
I am the captain of my soul.

Enough,   Masters-Captains-Teachers-Students-Readers—Doers All—as I list from 1 to 10 these ten thinking spurs, all based on Misesian self-interest, all holding the human mind is a terrible thing to waste:

1. Self-Thinker
2. Self-Causationist
3. Self-Constitutionalist
4. Self-Envisioner
5. Self-Competitor
6. Self-Realizer
7. Self-Lexiconist
8. Self-Expressionist
9. Self-Chooser
10. Self-Authorist

Now some wind-up thoughts on politics, on how the state acts in education and out, how we Americans sort out self-interests, including yours and mine. Sure, we 300 million Americans often have competitive interests and even spats, yet we often try to resolve differences by democracy.

Careful, Teachers-Students-Others. Note democracy takes two distinct, often opposed, formats. One is political democracy, rocky if not helter-skelter as well. For is it not also of a mostly coercive sort, one zero/negatively summed in overall benefit?

So savvy the wit in George Bernard Shaw's cut that the state that robs Peter to pay Paul can always count on the support of Paul.

Or savvy the fact that our Welfare-Warfare State has nothing to give but what it first taxes away, that welfarism and militarism sink into a shallow zero/negative sum game, a fruitless denial of economics' iron law of opportunity cost—i.e., No Free Lunch, No Something for Nothing.

For no matter what you or the state does, it is ever at the cost of something else, one foreclosing the other, as everyone seeks the most profitable option at hand, often by his/her immediate lights.

Everyone? Yes, allowing for mistakes, and for even those who profess to being anti-profit yet profit by their anti-profiteering.

Or else why would they do it?

Here see profit at base as utilitarian, as the pursuit of happiness à la Jefferson in the Declaration of Independence—not as something mercenary.

Look. Political democracy means majority rule, with usual push and shove by special interests, as the minority must go along.

Must? No wonder Thomas Paine in his *Common Sense* in 1776 said the state is "a necessary evil." So our Founders set the Bill of Rights, the First Ten Amendments, so to limit state power, so to save both the individual and the minority from a domineering majority. Some majority. Ponder . . .

H.L. Mencken and his punchy last word in his definition of democracy: "Democracy is the theory that the common people know what they want and deserve to get it good and hard."

For note today's government-imposed—however inadvertently—financial crisis borne by the U.S. and world today, how the U.S. bails out federally-sponsored lending giants Fannie Mae and Freddie Mac, partly nationalizes ten major banks, pumps many hundreds of billions of dollars into our sick economy, seeks to bail out the Big Three auto-makers of GM, Ford, and Chrysler, getting them to give up their corporate jets while providing a federal jet for House Speaker Nancy Pelosi. Consistency anyone?

I revert to Ralph Waldo Emerson once more when he said: "A foolish consistency is the hobgoblin of little minds."

All this is aimed at, audaciously, hopefully, economic salvation. Sure.

For isn't the catch of Obamanomics' stimulus and massive renewal of the nation's infrastructure that it is based on the very government which created problems, including today's bust, in the first place? Wasn't President Ronald Reagan on target when he said government is the problem—not the solution?

So economic trauma. Look about and ask: What happened to early Constitutional limits on inept, corruptive state power, on undoing that early Constitution's blockage of a federal income tax via permitting per capita head taxes only—undone by the Sixteenth Income Tax Amendment of 1913?

Or what happened to the gold standard—honest money so desperately needed by a sick world economy, by every American today and more so tomorrow?

Or as P.J. O'Rourke famously said: "Giving money and power to government is like giving whiskey and car keys to teenage boys."

Economic and other trauma too for our public K–12 schools dominated if not ruled by the powerful National Education Association and its 50 state chapters.

For does not forced education, loss of school competition and critical parent-student choice, much explain our high drop-out rates—about 33 percent nationally, with the District of Columbia worse off as 41 percent of its student body fail to earn a high school diploma.

Thus does D.C. schools chancellor Michelle Rhee have her schools pay middle students up to $100 a month to stay in school? I kid you not.

And don't those big drop-out rates rate an "F" grade for our K–12 national public school system? Or lower than the poor grades for those disheartened caught-up drop-outs—victims in a way of a fouled-up socialist system?

Now think of America's other democracy as market democracy. Think of our Second Democracy as gloriously voluntary, central to liberty, highly productive, positively-summed in mutual benefit, dubbed business, commerce, or, for us Teachers-Students-Parents, as private/semi-private education (charter schools).

Based on after-tax income—recall Chief Justice John Marshall's opinion in 1819 that "The power to tax involves the power to destroy"—this true democracy is true self-rule, true self-government at work, a vast 24/7 ongoing plebiscite of the entire world market system where your after-tax money and credit serve as daily ballots as we consumers choose producers.

Thus see at work in a market society—or what's left of it—consumer sovereignty, the neat phrase by Mises.

So consumers (including businesses in their own big consumer materials and manpower acquisition function) should not shun foreign producers offering bargains.

I say: Globalize more, seek greater international productivity, raise thereby the odds for World Peace Through World Trade (quite a thought, courtesy of IBM founder and its first CEO Thomas J. Watson).

Regarding education: Sure, consumers can choose among parochial and other private school producers including home schools, but watch out for that elephant in the living room swallowing up 89 percent the nation's school-age population. But 11 percent for our side.

Elephant?

Another analogy for the U.S. K–12 public school system is that it may be a sort of a Tower of Babel where communication between teachers and students tends to break down, as unsettling, some teacher union strikes break out across the country and large numbers of glum students give up and drop out.

Thus did Nobel economist Milton Friedman and his wife Rose put the bulk of their estate into the Friedman Foundation in Indianapolis with but one big goal:

> *Widen or restore parent-student choice*
> *via charters in our K–12 public schools*
> *and via vouchers for private schools.*

The Friedmans remind me of the wisdom of Mark Twain who declared: "I have never let my schooling interfere with my education."

As society votes to win what Mises student, Nobel economist F.A. Hayek called "spontaneous social cooperation," his phrase for free minds-free markets, for voluntarism-freedom of contract.

Recall Jefferson in 1776 saluting market democracy as part of Creator-endowed "Life, Liberty, and the Pursuit of Happiness," with Jefferson later warning us: "A government big enough to give you all you want is strong enough to take all you have."

Now, what of our "free" (ha!) public schools? Mises—leery of state-propagandizing/mind-control—hit any state role whatever in education: Zero. Zilch. As Mises warned us in *Liberalism*,1927:

> There is, in fact, only one solution: The state, the government, the laws must not in any way concern themselves with schooling or education. Public funds must not be used for such purposes. The rearing and instruction of youth must be left entirely to parents and to private associations and institutions. (p. 115)

To which, Dear Teachers, Dear Students, Dear Readers, I say, Amen, and Amen too, with bias, for the gist of my remarks today per an ancient saying, "As a man thinketh, so is he," Which I amend for our purpose: As a teacher-student-citizen thinketh, so is he/she.

To be continued. On and on. Why? Because of sharper thinking, our positive ideas tend to live: On and on, as their beacons—and hopefully yours, Dear Reader—light up future generations or far beyond everyone's own limited lease on life.

Not a bad deal, Dear Reader-Fellow Teachers-Fellow Students, not bad at all.